WOMEN

FROM "ADVENTURES AND CONFESSIONS"

BY

WILLIAM LYON PHELPS

British Library Cataloguing-in-Publication Data
A catalogue record for this book is available from the
British Library

Contents

William Lyon Phelps

William Lyon Phelps was born on 2nd January 1865, in New Haven, Conneticut, United States.

Phelps earned a B.A. in 1887, writing his thesis on the Idealism of George Berkeley. He then gained an M.A. in 1891 from Yale and his PhD from Harvard in the same year. During his time a Yale, he offered a course in modern novels which brought the university considerable attention both nationally and internationally. This was quite controversial at the time and Phelps was pressured to give up the course, but eventually, due to popular demand, reinstated it outside the official curriculum.

In 1892, Phelps married Annabel Hubbard, sister of childhood friend Frank Hubbard, and the couple moved to the family estate overlooking Lake Huron. Phelps christened it "The House of the Seven Gables", after the Nathanial Hawthorne story of the same name.

He became a very popular figure at Yale but also as an inspirational orator. He went on lecture tours that drew large audiences, speaking on the virtues of modern literature. He also preached regularly at the Huron City Methodist Episcopal Church and attracted such large crowds that the church was remodelled twice in five years to accommodate them.

Phelps published many essays on modern and European literature, including titles such as *Essays on Modern Novelists* (1910), *Some Makers of American Literature* (1923), and *As I Like it* (1923).

After his retirement from Yale in 1933, after 41 years of service, Phelps continued his public speaking, preaching, and writing a newspaper column. He also sat on book selection committees and acted as a judge for the Pulitzer Prize for literature.

His wife, Annabel, died from a stroke in 1939 and Phelps died four years later, in 1943.

WOMEN FROM "ADVENTURES AND CONFESSIONS"

It is high time that some preacher showed a little chivalry;

Although women are necessary to the welfare, progress and success of the Church, and although they are tireless workers in Church and Sunday School and tireless listeners to tiresome preachers, they seldom receive compliments from the pulpit. On the contrary: women are more often preached *at* than praised. Paul, who knew less about women than about anything else, was the first Christian minister to make the vain attempt of putting "woman in her place"; and many modern pastors, with no more knowledge, and considerably less ability, have embarked on the same fruitless and perilous enterprise. Women have been denounced from the pulpit for their hair, their hats, and their gowns; a subject of which the only man qualified to speak is not a clergyman, but a tailor.

It is high time that some preacher showed a little chivalry; and I, an amateur instead of a professional, will now do so. Women who read this sermon will find something to their advantage.

3

I like the retort made by a woman novelist to a critic. He: "Most women have no sense of humour. " She: "Well, what of it? Most men have *no sense at all.*" If this be true, it might be historically accounted for by the child's version of what happened in the Garden of Eden. "God made Adam and he was very lonely, so God put him to sleep, took out his brains and made a woman."

"Hope not for mind in woman," said the poet Donne; but when he wrote that, he was not looking for mind.

If an honest man is the noblest work of God, a good woman is the finest.

Fashions change, manners change, the idea of beauty in anatomy, architecture, and in all the arts changes, but characteristics of the ideal man; modesty, amiability, gentleness have always characterised the ideal woman.

Clever young women who think the surest way to popularity is through shock, would do well to remember that the essentials of character are the same in all times and places. I remember, in a once famous farce called *A Trip to Chinatown*, a dialogue between a pretty girl whose facial charm was exceeded only by her audacity, and an unscrupulous man of the world. She asked him several questions: "You find me beautiful? fascinating? Brilliant? You like to be with me?" To all of which enquiries she received an emphatic affirmative reply. Then she asked, "And you would like to marry me, would't you?" "Not for gold or precious stones."

If an honest man is the noblest work of God, a good woman is the finest.

Women were just as necessary to the early church as they are now.

It is a rather curious fact that in the Old Testament the most famous women are villains, and in the New Testament the leading woman characters are saintly. I need only mention Jezebel and Delilah: Athaliah, more terrible than an army with banners; after these sinister persons, come Jael the murderer, and Deborah who glorified the cowardly deed; even the lovely and charming Ruth excelled chiefly in what is a second-rate virtue, obedience. But the New Testament women are immortal in their spiritual beauty. Mary the immaculate mother of Jesus; Mary Magdalene, the reformed harlot; Martha and her sister Mary, the first representatives respectively of low and high church; the woman of Samaria who spread the news of the living water; the sick woman who touched the hem of Christ's garment; the poor widow who contributed all her fortune and her heart with it; the woman who was content with crumbs from the Master's table; the woman who publicly blessed Christ's mother; the women who followed Him to the cross, *stayed there,* and were the first to visit the tomb.

In addition to these, the work of Peter and of Paul could not have been successful without the support of woman. Women were just as necessary to the early church as they are now.

It is often said that the interests of women are petty;

I do not understand why the fact that more women than men go to church should be regarded as counting against its value. The fact itself is more damaging to the men who stay away than it is to the church; but why should an assemblage of persons where women predominate connote intellectual inferiority? One minister complained to another that he could not get men to come to his services; and asked for his advice. The other said, "Why last Sunday I preached to an enormous audience composed entirely of men." It was in the county jail.

The truth is that the proportionate worth of any undertaking is usually indicated by the excess of women over men who are interested in it. Firstclass music is surely not despicable; at orchestra concerts the women vastly outnumber the men. Art exhibitions are not for silly and stupid people; there are ten women to one man who show their interest by attendance. On the other hand, at a prize-fight the men still outnumber the women; and at a cock-fight I am informed there are scarcely any women at all, and those few disguised in men's clothes; so that their presence and support will seem natural.

It is often said that the interests of women are petty; that they read in the newspapers only the Social Column and the Fashion Page. Even if this is true, men's interests are hardly on a grander scale; for men will read with avidity five columns in fine print consisting of details connected with upper-cuts, left hooks, and side-stepping.

There is an instinct in women that leads them infallibly to choose and possess the best things in life.

It is just that women should support Christianity, for they owe their present independence more to Christianity than to anything else. Consider the position of women among Pagans, Mohammedans, American Indians, and heathen in general; and contrast that with their status in Christian countries. When Lafcadio Hearn lectured on English poetry to Japanese students at Tokio, he had considerable difficulty in explaining to them the conventional worshipful attitude maintained by English poets to women.

Women love religion, music, art, and poetry because they instinctively *know* that those things are immortal, whereas forms of government, politics, stock quotations, are ephemeral. Women do not have to be told that music and all forms of imperishable beauty are interesting; they *know* it. There is an instinct in women that leads them infallibly to choose and possess the best things in life.

Women do go forth to the scene of battle; but instead of going out to destroy, they go out to heal and restore.

If you wish to interest the average man in some enterprise, you must show him there is something in it making for his personal material advantage, or at all events for the practical welfare of the community; but the average woman will respond to an appeal based on beauty or nobility.

It used to be said by those opposed to granting political privileges to women, that in war they were anyhow inferior; for war was exclusively man's business. But since the days of Florence Nightingale – and even Lytton Strachey's adroit wit has not been able to darken her fame- we know that man has succeeded in making war the business of women. Women do go forth to the scene of battle; but instead of going out to destroy, they go out to heal and restore. The Red Cross, the Hospital Nurses, illustrate how women, by crucifying themselves, have saved men.

...men and women must learn from each other.

In *The Princess*, Tennyson, although old-fashioned and over conservative, was eternally right in insisting on the natural fact that woman and man are different. "Woman is not lesser man," but quite another thing. Thus the attempts of women to resemble men are as vain as they are silly. Why on earth should a woman want to be like a man? Yet Tennyson, in a few lines that should be read at every marriage-service, said that men and women must learn from each other.

Men should acquire sympathy and tenderness without losing virility; women should acquire understanding and the unprejudiced breadth of outlook that is born only of intelligence.

...let them think for themselves.

Women ought to cultivate their mental powers; much more than they do now. It is a true indictment against women that giving them the vote in national politics has produced no appreciable effect – which means that they have manifested no intellectual independence. There is no reason women should vote the same ticket as that voted by their husbands and fathers; let them think for themselves.

They have not, in the main, taken the privilege of the ballot seriously. They ought to qualify for citizenship by hard and faithful study of public questions. The League of Women Voters has done much; but there are more men today who can tell why they vote a certain ticket than there are women.

...the principle of development.

In his gossipy poem, *Old Pictures in Florence*, Browning makes a comparison between the perfection of Greek art and the imperfection of the human mind. He says that because Greek art is perfect, it reached its goal; it was finished; it therefore cannot develop. The human mind is faulty and clumsy, but it is *alive:* it has within its imperfections the principle of eternal development. Therefore when we look at perfect Greek statues, we should not repine because our bodies are so far short of the ideal human frame; we should rejoice, because with all our imperfections, nay because of our imperfections, our minds have something finer than any form of perfection – the principle of development.

...but every one can improve in mind and character.

Too many women are worried or despondent about minor matters, while they regard serious defect with complacency. It is of course important that they should look as well as possible, and dress as becomingly as their means will allow; but these are not the most serious considerations. Many women (and men) are keenly concerned about their looks and their clothes; am I looking my best tonight? are my clothes right? When really they should ask themselves, have I got any brains? and if not, how shall I supply this deficiency?

Every one, says Browning, looks at a perfect statue, and soliloquises, "Ah, I wish I looked like that!" a vain and impossible wish. It is difficult, by taking thought, that is, by worrying about it, to add a cubit to one's stature, or to change the curve of one's nose, or to acquire sudden wealth; but every one can improve in mind and character.

11

A heart whose love is innocent.

The Pope said of Pompilia that she was just as truly an angel living on earth, dressed in her street clothes, as she was in heaven, clad in radiant garments. Innocence in love, beauty of aspiration, cleanliness of heart, often increase facial beauty. Byron, who had had sufficient experience of light women, reserved his highest tribute for carefree innocence and noble impulses.

She walks in beauty, like the night
Of cloudless climes and starry skies,
And all that's best of dark and bright
Meets in her aspect and her eyes,
Thus mellow'd to that tender light
Which heaven to gaudy day denies.

One shade the more, one ray the less
Had half impair'd the nameless grace
Which waves in every raven tress
Or softly lightens o'er her face,
Where thoughts serenely sweet express
How pure, how dear their dwelling place.

And on that cheek and o'er that brow
So soft, so calm, yet eloquent,

The smiles that win, the tints that glow
But tell of days in goodness spent,-
A mind at peace with all below,
A heart whose love is innocent.

A perfect woman, nobly plann'd

Byron's great contemporary, Wordsworth, showed in one of his finest tributes to women that their attractiveness did not depend on romantic illusion; that with the right sort of wife and mother, daily intimacy did not lessen personal charm.

I hope that Hawthorne did not intend his character Hilda, in *The Marble Faun*, to be the ideal woman; for toward Hilda I cannot repress a feeling of aversion. "Her soul was like a star and dwelt apart"; but from the selfish sanctity of its seclusion, no real good resulted; no one was aided or comforted or inspired in the struggle of life. She was no help to sinners; she was their despair. She had the purity of an angel, but not the purity of a good woman. She was like one who should refuse to help a drowning man, for fear of soiling her clothes.

But Wordsworth showed that a good woman need not lose her ideality or her romantic, mysterious attraction, even in the daily household duties. She could be practical,

sagacious, efficient; and yet have the fascination of a nymph
in the moonlight.

> She was a phantom of delight
> When first she gleam'd upon my sight;
> A lovely apparition, sent
> To be a moment's ornament;
> Her eyes as stars of twilight fair;
> Like Twilight's, too, her dusky hair;
> But all things else about her drawn
> From May-time and the cheerful dawn;
> A dancing shape, an image gay,
> To haunt, to startle, and waylay.
>
> I saw her upon nearer view,
> A spirit, yet a woman too!
> Her household motions light and free,
> And steps of virgin-liberty;
> A countenance in which did meet
> Sweet records, promises as sweet;
> A creature not too bright or good
> For Human nature's daily food,
> For transient sorrows, simple wiles,
> Praise, blame, love, kisses, tears, and smiles.

And now I see with eye serene
The very pulse of the machine;
A being breathing thoughtful breath,
A traveller between life and death;
The reason firm, the temperate will,
Endurance, foresight, strength, and skill;
A perfect woman, nobly plann'd
To warm, to comfort, and command;
And yet a Spirit still, and bright
With something of an angel-light.

Little girls ... surpass boys in one important respect; their *ideals* are good.

There is no doubt that the average man has more physical strength than the average woman; it does not occur to any sensible woman to be ashamed of this inferiority. Well, history seems to show that in matters of initiative, in creative and administrative powers, the average man is again superior to the average woman. I cannot see why any woman should resent this any more than she resents her lack of physical strength.

For in the love of beauty, in ideality, in refinement, in purity, in accuracy of *feeling*, women are as superior to men as they are inferior in brute force. The best way to observe this is to consider children.

The instincts of the average healthy boy are mainly bad. Robbers and murderers are his heroes. In primary schools - not in college - the toughest boy is the idol of the others. I remember when I was six years old, there was in our room at school an absolute young villain, who would have destroyed the world, had he possessed sufficient power. He was vulgar, foul, pugnacious, cruel, and a bully; he was our hero. (He is now, I believe, in prison.) One day I was behaving badly, and some one said to me, "Why, if you go on in this way, you will be like Blank!" My eyes glowed with delight. He was my ideal!

The only way boys - who are savages at heart - become decent citizens and fit to live with - is through discipline, corporal punishment, public opinion, and the grace of God.

Little girls - very little - while they are not angelic, and may betray meanness and pettiness, surpass boys in one important respect; their *ideals* are good. They do not want to grow up and become adventuresses and scoundrels, they want to do good, help the sick and needy, stimulate the best impulses of men.

I happen to know the real value of the work done by women, and their sacrifices.

So many women have longed to be of use to men, have considered it their highest happiness to influence men in right directions, that the careers of many successful men have been accompanied by the sacrifice of women who could not bear to "stand in their way." I once saw a double-page picture in *Life*. It represented a vast space of deep water; a woman was drowning; all that was visible of her sinking body was her two hands above the surface; a few yards distant, a strong man was rapidly swimming *away from her;* and under the picture was the one word *Success.*

Many of our modern novelists love to expend their talents for ridicule and satire on evangelical churches, and especially on the organisations of women who do most of the work; the Ladies' Aid Society, the Foreign Mission Band, the Sewing Circle, and so on. Now three months of the year, I am associated with a small country church in a mid-western state (Huron City, Michigan). I happen to know the real value of the work done by women, and their sacrifices. In addition to the housework, they have to wash and dress the children, and from afar bring them to church and Sunday School; they do all this because they know the value of religion in daily life; they are not going to have their children brought up in ignorance and savagery.

I hope that in heaven God reserves an especially comfortable chair for the oldest daughter in a large family. This girl has no youth; from her earliest recollection she has always had to "mind the baby." She has to clean up after the younger ones, doing all the drudgery of a mother with none of the maternal passion that glorifies it.

Stabat Mater

Women not only have more passive courage than men, such as waiting in solitary anxiety, with none of the relief that action brings. They often have more of the desperate, reckless courage, that goes with the love of adventure. Marriage is an enterprise filled with more peril for a woman than for a man; a woman leaves the security of her home, and takes a chance with a stranger. No children would ever be born if men had to bear them; no man could stand the months of inactivity and sickness, with horrible agony and mortal danger as the climax. And if everything then turns out successfully, for three years the mother must know every instant in the twenty-four hours of every day, exactly where that child is. Are we men really worth all that agony and fatigue and boredom?

Well, there are some men who appreciate their mothers and their wives. They appreciate their mothers after the mothers are dead; and they appreciate their wives when they, the men, are sick.

The position of women as home-makers is also appreciated by some bachelors. The great Russian novelist, Turgenev, whom George Moore called the greatest artist since antiquity, said, "I would give up all my fame and all my art if there were one woman who cared whether or not I came home late to dinner."

The *Stabat Mater* applies not only to the mother of Jesus at the cross, it applies to millions of women who have "stood by" their husbands and their sons. The capacity of women to "stand by" can never be overestimated; that is why it is such an irreparable disaster for a man to lose his mother. A boy may be common-place, even stupid, the butt of his schoolfellows; but there is a woman at home in whose eyes he is a romantic hero; one who idealises him; one to whom he will never turn in vain.